Your Culture Isn't Broken.

Your Leadership Is.

The Hidden Leadership Mistakes That Destroy Workplace Culture

Your Culture Isn't Broken.

Your Leadership is.

The Hidden Leadership Mistakes That Destroy Workplace Culture

Katie Simpson

Copyright

Published in the United States by **Ember & Oak Consulting LLC**, Montana
For inquiries, visit www.katiesimpsonbooks.com

ISBN: 979-8-9931490-7-3
Cover design by Katie Simpson
Printed in the United States of America

First Edition

Also by Katie Simpson

Nonfiction & Workplace Culture

Your Culture Isn't Broken. Your Leadership Is.
A direct look at why workplace dysfunction persists—and how real
leadership accountability can fix it.

Humor & Life Reflections

Lower Your Expectations (and Other Life Skills)
A sarcastic survival guide to adulthood, modern life, and the strange
expectations we place on ourselves.

The Joy of Not Giving a Damn
A humorous and honest reminder that peace often begins the
moment you stop carrying everyone else's nonsense.

Well, That Was Enlightening
Stories, reflections, and moments of clarity that arrive when life
refuses to follow the plan.

Family & Personal Legacy

Love Letters to My Children
A heartfelt collection of reflections, life lessons, and stories written
for the next generation.

Ken & Chaos: A Love Story
A humorous and deeply personal look at marriage, resilience, and
building a life together through the unexpected.

More books, articles, and updates can be found at:
www.katiesimpsonbooks.com

Table of Contents

Dedication

To everyone who's ever carried a team on their back, held things together when leadership fell apart, and laughed through the chaos just to survive another day, this is for you.

And especially to my favorite leaders, you know who you are because you are the ones that set the bar high.

For the quiet truth-tellers, the behind-the-scenes heroes, the ones who do the real work while the meetings multiply and the slogans get shinier.

You are the reason workplaces still function. You are the heartbeat of every company that forgot to say thank you.

May you always find humor in the madness, courage in the dysfunction, and workplaces that finally deserve your brilliance.

Acknowledgments

Writing a book like this means sifting through years of chaos, calling out dysfunction, and reflecting on what happens when leadership loses its way. But it also means remembering the good—the people who made it bearable, the ones who proved that respect and decency still exist.

To the rare leaders who got it right: thank you. You showed me that integrity isn't a buzzword, that fairness can coexist with accountability, and that leadership done right can change everything. You are the proof that not all hope is lost.

To every coworker, friend, and fellow survivor who kept their humor alive in places that didn't deserve it, thank you for the laughter. You reminded me that humor isn't avoidance; it's endurance.

And to the people still searching for a workplace that matches their effort, that honors their integrity, that treats them like human beings, I see you. I wrote this for you.

Finally, to the good companies, the ones that still understand that culture isn't a campaign, it's a commitment. Thank you for reminding us what's possible when leadership chooses people over ego.

Preface

Leadership books are everywhere.

Every year, another stack appears promising the secret formula for building great teams, inspiring employees, and transforming workplace culture. Most of them follow the same pattern. Someone reaches the corner office, reflects on their journey, and packages their experience into a framework, a philosophy, or a tidy set of principles meant to explain how leadership should work.

But most of those books are written from the top of the organizational chart.

This one isn't.

This book is written from the floor, where the real work happens. It comes from years of watching how organizations actually operate, not how leadership presentations claim they operate. It comes from observing the people who quietly keep businesses running while navigating systems that often make their work harder than it needs to be.

Over time, I began to notice something interesting. Whenever a workplace started to struggle, leadership rarely looked inward. Instead, the conversation always seemed to focus on culture. Consultants were hired. Mission statements were rewritten. New initiatives appeared promising to "rebuild engagement" or "strengthen workplace culture."

And yet, the underlying problems rarely changed.

Because most of the time, culture isn't the problem.

Leadership is.

When leadership drifts away from accountability, fairness, and honesty, culture inevitably follows. Employees see it immediately. They see the gap between what leadership says and what leadership does. They see the double standards, the buzzwords that replace clarity, and the decisions that quietly erode trust.

Eventually, they stop pretending everything is fine.

This book is not a traditional leadership manual. It does not present a complicated framework or a revolutionary new theory. Instead, it holds up a mirror to the modern workplace. It reflects the meetings that accomplish nothing, the corporate language that hides confusion, and the leadership habits that slowly drain morale from otherwise capable teams.

If you are an employee reading this, you will probably recognize many of these situations. You may even find yourself nodding along to moments that feel painfully familiar.

If you are a leader reading this, some parts of this book may be uncomfortable. That discomfort is not the goal, but it may be unavoidable. Honest conversations about leadership often are.

The truth is that most people do not hate work. In fact, most people genuinely want to contribute, solve problems, and take pride in what they do. What they struggle with is dysfunction. They struggle with systems that create unnecessary obstacles and leadership that confuses activity with progress.

Burnout rarely comes from effort alone. It comes from spending too much energy navigating broken systems while pretending those systems are working.

This book is about speaking that truth out loud.

It explores the everyday realities employees experience but often feel discouraged from discussing openly: the meetings that lead nowhere, the promotions that reward the wrong people, the policies that exist on paper but not in practice, and the quiet frustration that builds when leadership refuses to acknowledge what everyone else can clearly see.

At the same time, this book is not simply a critique. Good leadership does exist. It may not always be loud or flashy, but when it appears, it changes everything. Strong leaders create environments where people feel respected, supported, and trusted to do their work well.

Real leadership does not require complicated theories. It rests on a few simple ideas practiced consistently: telling the truth, treating people fairly, taking responsibility for decisions, and holding everyone to the same standards.

When leaders do those things, culture improves naturally. When they do not, no amount of slogans or motivational campaigns will repair the damage.

This book is not about reinventing leadership.

It is about remembering what leadership was supposed to be in the first place.

Most companies think they have a culture problem.

They don't.

They have a leadership problem.

Chapter 1: Why We're All Exhausted

Work isn't the problem. Most people actually want to work. We want to build something, solve problems, contribute, and feel proud of what we do at the end of the day. What wears people down isn't effort. It's the mountain of dysfunction dumped on top of the work: chaos disguised as culture, control disguised as leadership, and corporate theater somehow passed off as strategy.

People are not exhausted because work is hard. They're exhausted because too many workplaces make hard work harder than it needs to be.

Everywhere you look, dysfunction is running the show. Meetings multiply like rabbits but never lead to decisions. Leaders hover over tiny details while missing the big picture entirely. HR too often operates like a complaint intake desk with a party-planning side hustle. Buzzwords pile up so thick you need a machete just to find the truth.

It's not the work that drains people. It's the nonsense surrounding the work: broken systems, weak leadership, pointless bureaucracy, and the steady drip of disrespect baked into everyday decisions.

Take micromanagement disguised as "security." I once worked for a company that recorded everything: calls, meetings, chat messages — all of it. At first glance, it sounded like accountability. It wasn't. Leadership didn't want clarity. They wanted control. They wanted dirt. And nothing destroys trust faster than realizing every word you say might be twisted into ammunition later. That wasn't transparency. That was corporate surveillance with a superiority complex.

Then there are the strategic planning meetings. I once sat through a three-hour meeting where nobody left with an actual plan. Leadership congratulated themselves for being "aligned." Aligned with what, exactly? Nobody knew. Employees walked out more confused than when they came in, while the executives acted like they had just solved world hunger. That wasn't strategy. That was theater.

And if you've worked in high-pressure industries like mortgage, finance, or sales, you've seen a special flavor of this madness. One quarter it's all growth, urgency, and "let's hire as fast as possible." The next quarter the market shifts, volume tightens, and the same leaders who acted invincible start slashing jobs, overloading the survivors, and calling it discipline. The people doing the real work are expected to absorb the chaos without flinching. That's not resilience. That's organizational whiplash.

Executives love to tell themselves employees leave because they're lazy, entitled, or ungrateful. Wrong. Employees leave because they're drowning in impossible expectations, unsupported by the very people paid to lead them. Good employees do not run from hard work. They run from dysfunction dressed up as ambition.

The cost of that dysfunction is bigger than most leaders want to admit. It erodes trust. Once trust goes, your best people stop giving you their best. They stop caring. They stop speaking up. Then they start looking for the door. And when they leave, they take their momentum, judgment, creativity, and sanity with them — none of which can be replaced by another pizza party, morale email, or culture initiative.

Dysfunction is expensive. It costs morale, productivity, credibility, retention, and reputation. You can keep recycling the same broken playbook, the same empty buzzwords, the same recycled managers, but eventually people stop pretending it's normal.

Exhaustion does not come from effort. It comes from disrespect.

People can handle hard work. What they cannot handle is being ignored, manipulated, micromanaged, and treated like tools with expiration dates.

Employees are not worn out by the job itself. They are worn out by the broken leadership wrapped around it.

And if executives don't start paying attention, one day they'll look around and realize the people are gone, the energy is gone, and all that's left is an empty culture deck explaining why no one stayed.

Chapter 2: Corporate BS Bingo

If you've ever sat through a corporate meeting and thought you needed subtitles, congratulations—you've already played Corporate BS Bingo.

Somewhere in offices across the country, employees are sitting in conference rooms nodding politely while mentally checking off squares on an imaginary bingo card. "Synergy." Check. "Strategic pivot." Check. "Low-hanging fruit." Check. Someone in the back quietly whispers "Bingo," and suddenly the only genuine laughter in the meeting appears.

Nothing erodes credibility faster than jargon. When leaders don't have clear answers, many of them reach for buzzwords the way magicians reach for smoke and mirrors. The hope is that the language sounds impressive enough that nobody notices nothing meaningful was actually said.

Meanwhile, employees sit quietly around the table, nodding politely while mentally filling out an imaginary bingo card.

Every workplace has its own collection of these phrases, but the classics show up almost everywhere.

"We're a family."
Translation: We expect unconditional loyalty right up until the moment layoffs become convenient.

"We value transparency."
Translation: You will receive a carefully edited portion of the truth.

"This is a business decision."
Translation: You're not going to like what happens next, but please pretend you understand.

"We need team players."
Translation: We are about to ask you to do three jobs for one paycheck.

"We're restructuring."
Translation: We don't actually know what we're doing, but moving people around makes it look like we do.

The language always sounds polished and strategic. The effect, however, is usually the opposite. Instead of inspiring confidence, it leaves employees confused and skeptical. People find themselves translating corporate code just to figure out what leadership actually means.

And once the buzzwords start flowing, they tend to multiply quickly. Suddenly everyone is "circling back," "leveraging synergies," "driving alignment," and "pivoting strategically." At some point the conversation starts sounding less like a business discussion and more like a corporate-themed game of Mad Libs.

Employees know when language is being used as camouflage. Leaders sometimes believe that dressing uncomfortable news in softer language will make it easier to accept. In reality, it often has the opposite effect. The more polished the message becomes, the more obvious it is that something is being hidden.

I once worked for a company that hired a new executive with great fanfare. Within two weeks, the entire department was called into an all-hands meeting so the new leader could present their "vision" for the future.

The presentation included all the usual highlights: synergy, alignment, optimization, and a promise that we were entering a bold new chapter.

By Friday, half the department had been laid off.

That wasn't a bold new chapter. That was a bloodbath wrapped in PowerPoint slides.

Employees walked out stunned and angry, while leadership congratulated themselves on how well they had communicated the change. That moment captures Corporate BS Bingo perfectly: dress up a disaster in polished language and hope nobody notices the difference.

And the phrases never stop evolving.

"We're optimizing headcount."
Translation: We overhired and now you're paying the price.

"We're implementing new efficiencies."
Translation: Your team of five is now a team of two.

"We're evolving our brand identity."
Translation: We changed the logo.

"Let's circle back."
Translation: We will never discuss this again.

Eventually, employees begin coping with the absurdity through humor. Some teams literally create bingo cards filled with corporate buzzwords and mark them off during meetings. Words like bandwidth, low-hanging fruit, synergy, and strategic pivot get crossed off in real time while executives continue speaking, convinced they are delivering a masterclass in leadership.

The only people not in on the joke are the people running the meeting.

And that humor is more than sarcasm. It is a warning sign.

When employees start joking about leadership instead of listening to leadership, credibility is already slipping away. Humor becomes a coping mechanism, a way to survive environments where honest communication has quietly disappeared.

Leaders sometimes confuse polished language with professionalism. They believe sounding "executive" is the same as being clear. In reality, most employees would gladly trade the buzzwords for a few simple sentences that explain what is actually happening.

People can handle difficult news. They can handle layoffs, market downturns, and strategic changes. What they struggle with is being spun. When layoffs are called "realignment," employees do not feel reassured—they feel insulted.

I once heard a CEO announce a large round of layoffs by saying, "We're excited about the opportunities this will create for our future."

Excited.

Hundreds of people had just lost their jobs, and the official tone was excitement. That wasn't leadership. That was corporate theater delivered with a smile.

Executives need to understand something important: employees rarely roll their eyes at bad news. They roll their eyes at obvious nonsense. If layoffs are coming, say layoffs. If the market is difficult, say the market is difficult. If mistakes were made, admit the mistakes.

Plain language builds trust. Spin destroys it.

If you want the next meeting to actually matter, start by speaking like a human being. Tell people what is happening, why it is happening, and how it affects them. Skip the buzzwords. Skip the theatrical language. Say what you mean.

Because if your team is quietly playing Corporate BS Bingo while you're talking, they are not listening.

They are surviving.

And when employees are just surviving meetings instead of learning from them, your culture is already in trouble.

When meetings turn into memes, leadership has already lost the room.

Chapter 3: The Leadership Problem

Every company talks about culture.

Very few talk honestly about leadership.

But here's the uncomfortable truth: most workplaces don't actually have a culture problem. They have a leadership problem.

Culture is the result of leadership behavior. It reflects the decisions leaders make, the standards they enforce, and the behavior they tolerate. When leadership works well, culture tends to stabilize naturally. When leadership fails, culture collapses quickly.

Good leaders are surprisingly quiet. They set clear expectations, provide the resources their teams need, and trust people to do their jobs. When problems arise, they step in to help solve them. When things go well, they step aside and let the team take the credit.

Bad leaders operate very differently.

They arrive with authority but very little self-awareness. They confuse control with competence and visibility with effectiveness. Instead of building strong teams, they drain energy from the people around them.

Over time, most employees learn to recognize the familiar leadership archetypes that appear in nearly every workplace.

There is the Micromanager, who treats every decision as if it requires their personal approval. Their constant oversight slowly suffocates initiative and creativity.

There is the Ghost, who disappears the moment things become difficult. When a crisis appears, the team is left scrambling while the leader suddenly becomes unavailable. Once the problem is solved, however, they reappear just in time to take credit.

There is the Bully, who believes intimidation is a legitimate management strategy. They raise their voice, belittle employees, and mistake silence for respect.

There is the Credit Thief, who quietly absorbs recognition for work they had little to do with while allowing others to take the blame when things go wrong.

And then there is the Oversharer, who turns the workplace into a personal therapy session that no one asked to attend.

Any one of these leadership styles can damage a team. When multiple traits appear in the same manager, the results can be catastrophic.

I once worked for a manager who somehow managed to combine several of these traits at once.

In meetings, they would casually gossip about employees to win loyalty from others. If someone questioned a decision, the tone changed instantly. Voices got louder. The room got quiet.

Problems were always someone else's fault. When a project succeeded, they stepped forward to explain their "leadership." When something failed, they vanished until the issue was resolved — then returned just in time to explain what everyone else should have done differently.

Employees learned the pattern quickly.

People stopped offering ideas. Conversations became cautious. Eventually the most capable employees simply left.

Eventually a lawsuit followed.

The company's response was not to examine the leadership problem. Instead, they protected the manager and blamed the turnover on "market conditions."

This happens more often than organizations want to admit.

Companies frequently promote employees into management roles because they were strong individual performers or because they had been with the company the longest. Unfortunately, success in a technical role does not automatically translate into leadership ability.

Leadership is not a reward for tenure. It is not a perk for political connections. It is not a family inheritance passed down to the boss's favorite employee.

Leadership is responsibility.

When organizations give authority to people who lack the ability or temperament to lead others, the consequences spread quickly. Morale declines. Trust erodes. Turnover increases. Eventually the entire culture begins to unravel.

And yet many companies continue to treat leadership development as an afterthought.

Executives invest heavily in innovation, marketing, and expansion while ignoring the one factor that determines whether those efforts succeed or fail: the quality of the people leading the organization.

Leadership failure rarely appears overnight. It builds slowly through small decisions. Protecting a toxic manager because they generate revenue. Promoting someone who lacks people skills because they are convenient. Ignoring employee concerns because addressing them would be uncomfortable.

Each of those choices sends a message. And employees are always paying attention.

Over time, people begin to understand what their organization truly values. Not the values printed on the website, but the values demonstrated through leadership behavior.

If accountability only applies to certain people, employees notice.

If bad managers face no consequences, employees notice.

If leadership talks about integrity but rewards favoritism, employees notice.

Eventually those observations turn into quiet conclusions about the workplace.

And once employees reach those conclusions, culture begins to deteriorate quickly.

Companies often spend enormous energy trying to repair culture without addressing the leadership behavior that created the problem in the first place.

But culture cannot be repaired until leadership is.

Chapter 4: Signs You Shouldn't Be a Manager

Not everyone belongs in management.

That statement shouldn't be controversial, but in many organizations it somehow is. Companies often treat management roles as the next logical step for high-performing employees. Someone excels in a technical role, consistently delivers results, and demonstrates deep knowledge of the work. Leadership assumes the obvious next move is to put them in charge of other people.

Unfortunately, that assumption is often wrong.

Being great at the work and being great at leading people are two completely different skills. One requires expertise and discipline. The other requires communication, emotional intelligence, and the ability to guide a group of individuals toward a shared goal. When organizations confuse the two, they end up promoting talented experts into roles that make everyone miserable—including the expert.

Leadership is not a promotion. It is permission. The moment people stop believing in the person leading them, the title stops meaning anything.

One of the most common management disasters begins with what I call the Incompetent Promoted Expert. This is the employee who was exceptional in their original role. They knew the systems inside and out, could solve problems faster than anyone else, and often became the person everyone turned to when things went sideways.

Naturally, leadership assumes that the best technical performer will also be the best leader.

So they promote them.

At first the decision seems logical. After all, if someone understands the work better than anyone else, surely they should be the person guiding the team.

Then reality sets in.

Suddenly the expert is responsible not just for their own work, but for the performance of an entire group. Instead of solving problems themselves, they now have to coach others through solving them. Instead of focusing on details, they must step back and see the broader picture.

For some people, that transition works. For many others, it does not.

The promoted expert often responds in the only way they know how: by doing the work themselves. They jump in to fix every issue, rewrite every report, and correct every small mistake. Their intention is usually good—they want things done correctly. But the effect is predictable. The team becomes hesitant, disengaged, and overly dependent on the manager to handle every decision.

Before long, the team stops learning because the manager never allows them to.

I once watched this happen in a department where the most knowledgeable employee had been promoted to lead the team. On paper it looked like a perfect choice. This person knew the systems better than anyone else and had years of experience navigating the company's processes.

But once they became the manager, something changed.

Instead of guiding the team, they began correcting everything. Every email was rewritten. Every decision required approval. Every task was reviewed down to the smallest detail. What had once been a capable team slowly turned into a group of people waiting for instructions.

The irony was that the new manager was working harder than ever. They were staying late, answering every question personally, and constantly jumping into the work.

From leadership's perspective, they looked incredibly dedicated.

From the team's perspective, they were suffocating the department.

Within a year, half the group had quietly started looking for other jobs.

The promoted expert wasn't a bad person. They weren't lazy or malicious. They had simply been placed in a role that required an entirely different skill set than the one that had made them successful.

Unfortunately, organizations repeat this mistake constantly.

Instead of asking whether someone wants to lead people, companies assume the next step in a career path must always be management. Instead of developing leadership skills, they hand someone a title and hope the rest works itself out.

Sometimes it does.

Often it does not.

There are other warning signs that someone should not be managing people.

If you cannot trust your team to make decisions without constant oversight, you are not managing—you are suffocating initiative.

If you avoid difficult conversations because they make you uncomfortable, problems will grow until they explode.

If you see employees as "resources" instead of individuals with skills, ambitions, and lives outside of work, you are already leading in the wrong direction.

And if you genuinely do not enjoy working with people, management is probably the last job you should have.

Leadership is not a reward for tenure. It is not a consolation prize for someone who might leave if they are not promoted. And it certainly should not be treated as the default career path for every strong performer.

Organizations that promote the wrong people into management roles eventually pay the price. Morale declines. Turnover rises. Productivity slows as teams struggle under leadership that was never prepared for the responsibility.

The tragedy is that the promoted expert often loses as well. Instead of continuing to excel in the role they once loved, they find themselves trapped in a position that drains their energy and frustrates the people around them.

A great individual contributor is incredibly valuable. Companies should celebrate that strength instead of forcing it into a management role it was never meant to fill.

Because the moment leadership becomes a reward instead of a responsibility, the damage spreads quickly.

And once employees realize that the person running the team has no idea how to lead it, the countdown to turnover has already begun.

Chapter 5: The Rise of the Unqualified

If you've ever sat in a meeting and thought, *How on earth did that person end up in charge?* you're not alone.

Corporate life has a long and proud tradition of promoting the wrong people.

On paper, companies insist that leadership roles are earned through performance, experience, and demonstrated ability. In reality, promotions often follow a very different formula—one based less on competence and more on convenience, familiarity, or proximity to the right people.

The result is the steady rise of the unqualified.

Instead of promoting the employees who quietly keep the company running, organizations frequently elevate the people who are most visible, most connected, or simply closest to the existing leadership circle.

Sometimes the problem looks like politics. Sometimes it looks like networking. And in certain industries, it looks like something even more predictable.

It looks like family.

Or friends.

In many workplaces—especially smaller companies or rapidly growing organizations—the leadership pipeline becomes surprisingly informal. Someone needs a new manager, a department head, or a vice president. Instead of conducting a thoughtful search for the best candidate, leadership turns to someone they already know.

A former colleague.
A friend from another company.
A cousin.
A spouse.
A golfing buddy who "knows the business."

Suddenly a leadership role appears, and the job description seems to match that person's résumé perfectly.

At least on paper.

Industries like mortgage lending provide a perfect environment for this dynamic. The business moves fast, relationships matter, and companies often grow quickly during strong markets. When volume spikes, leaders scramble to expand teams and fill management roles as quickly as possible.

And when speed becomes the priority, objectivity often disappears.

Instead of carefully evaluating who has the skills to lead people, leadership falls back on the simplest decision available: hiring someone they trust personally.

Trust is valuable, of course. But trust alone does not create competence.

I've watched organizations bring in friends of senior leaders and install them directly into management roles—sometimes with little understanding of the actual work their teams performed. On paper these hires looked impressive. They were described as experienced operators, strategic thinkers, or industry veterans.

In practice, the results were very different.

The new leader often spent their first months trying to understand the basics of the department while the employees beneath them quietly carried the workload. Decisions slowed down because the manager lacked context. Processes became inconsistent because leadership didn't understand how they worked.

Meanwhile, the rest of the team could see exactly what had happened.

This wasn't a promotion based on merit.

It was a relationship hire.

And nothing destroys morale faster than realizing the rules are different for certain people.

Employees who spent years building expertise suddenly find themselves reporting to someone who skipped the line entirely. Promotions that once seemed achievable now feel predetermined. Hard work begins to feel less like a path forward and more like a performance staged for leadership's convenience.

When that realization spreads through a team, motivation starts to erode quickly.

Why invest extra effort if advancement depends more on personal connections than actual ability?

Why develop expertise if leadership roles are handed out through relationships instead of results?

Organizations often underestimate how quickly employees recognize these patterns. People may not say anything publicly, but they notice when a leader's best qualification is their personal relationship with someone higher up the ladder.

And they talk about it.

Not in meetings. Not in official feedback sessions.

But quietly—over coffee, in hallway conversations, and in group chats that leadership will never see.

Once employees believe the system is rigged, engagement drops fast. The best performers start exploring opportunities elsewhere, while the ones who remain begin doing the minimum required to get through the day.

Leadership, meanwhile, often struggles to understand what went wrong.

They blame the market.
They blame the talent pool.
They blame a supposed lack of work ethic.

What they rarely examine is the decision that started the problem in the first place: placing the wrong person in charge.

To be clear, hiring someone you know is not automatically a mistake. Many strong leaders bring trusted colleagues with them when they move to new organizations. The difference is that those individuals still need to earn credibility through their performance.

Relationships may open doors.

Competence has to keep them open.

When organizations forget that distinction, the consequences ripple outward. Teams become frustrated. Productivity slows. Turnover quietly increases as experienced employees decide their future lies somewhere else.

By the time leadership recognizes the damage, the strongest people are already gone.

And the unqualified leader is still sitting in the corner office, wondering why the team seems so disengaged.

Promotions send a message about what an organization truly values. If leadership roles consistently go to the most capable people, employees will work hard to earn them.

But if promotions repeatedly favor the most connected individuals, the message becomes just as clear.

Performance is optional.

Relationships are not.

And once that message takes hold, rebuilding trust becomes far harder than protecting it in the first place.

Chapter 6: The Cost of Cutting Corners

In business, there is always pressure to move faster.

Sometimes that pressure comes from investors who expect steady growth. Sometimes it comes from executives chasing ambitious quarterly targets. And sometimes it comes from simple impatience— the belief that success belongs to the organization that moves the quickest.

At first, the shortcuts that follow rarely seem dramatic. A small policy exception here. A rushed review there. A subtle push to "find a way" when a situation doesn't fit perfectly within established guidelines.

Most of these decisions appear harmless in the moment. They are framed as flexibility, adaptability, or a willingness to move quickly in a competitive environment.

But shortcuts have a way of multiplying.

Once an organization begins treating its guardrails as optional, exceptions start appearing everywhere. What began as a rare accommodation slowly becomes a pattern. Processes designed to protect the company begin to look like obstacles standing in the way of speed.

And once speed becomes the primary goal, discipline often disappears.

This pattern becomes especially visible in industries that move quickly and operate under constant production pressure. Mortgage lending is one of them.

During strong markets, loan volume can surge rapidly. Pipelines expand. Teams scramble to keep up with the influx of files. Leadership celebrates record numbers while encouraging departments to move even faster.

Efficiency becomes the buzzword of the moment.

Underwriting timelines shrink. Reviews become compressed. Compliance processes that once felt essential begin to feel inconvenient. The unspoken message spreads through the organization: keep the pipeline moving.

Nobody explicitly says to ignore the rules. Instead, the language becomes softer.

"Let's see if there's a way to make this work."

"Is there some flexibility here?"

"Maybe we can take another look."

Employees understand what those phrases mean. When leadership is focused on speed, careful evaluation starts to feel like resistance. People begin searching for solutions that will keep the deal alive rather than asking the harder question of whether the deal should move forward at all.

At the same time, many organizations begin expanding aggressively to handle the increased workload. During boom cycles, companies hire quickly. Departments grow almost overnight. New roles appear, new teams are formed, and the company begins to feel unstoppable.

For a while, the momentum is real.

But markets rarely remain hot forever.

When conditions tighten—as they always eventually do—the same companies that hired rapidly suddenly find themselves facing shrinking pipelines and rising costs. Leadership begins searching for ways to restore profitability.

Departments shrink just as quickly as they expanded.

Entire teams disappear.

The employees who remain inherit the responsibilities of the ones who left.

The message changes again.

Do more with less.

Be efficient.

Work faster.

From the outside, this looks like financial discipline. From the inside, employees experience something very different. Workloads increase dramatically while resources shrink. Teams that were already moving at full speed are now expected to accelerate even further.

Production expectations rarely adjust to reflect reality. Leadership still expects the same numbers—or higher—even though fewer people remain to complete the work.

Eventually something has to give.

Files move through the system faster than they should. Reviews that once required careful analysis now happen in minutes. Decisions that deserve thoughtful discussion are rushed because nobody has the time to examine them properly.

In the short term, the organization may still appear successful. Deals continue closing. Revenue continues flowing. Leadership points to the numbers as evidence that everything is working.

But beneath the surface, the foundation is weakening.

Another problem begins to emerge during these periods of intense pressure: time itself becomes negotiable.

As workloads grow and staff shrinks, managers are often told that overtime is not an option. Labor budgets are tight, and leadership expects departments to maintain productivity without increasing payroll costs.

On paper, the instruction seems straightforward.

Control overtime. Maintain output.

But the work itself does not disappear simply because overtime has been restricted. Deadlines still exist. Clients still expect responses. Files still need to be reviewed, processed, and finalized.

So employees begin solving the problem in the only way available to them.

They work off the clock.

Sometimes it starts innocently enough. Someone logs in early to clear part of the backlog before the day officially begins. Another finishes reviewing files from home at night because the pipeline was too heavy during business hours. Someone answers emails after dinner because waiting until morning would slow the process down.

At first, these choices feel like dedication. Employees tell themselves they are simply staying on top of their responsibilities.

But over time, the behavior spreads.

What began as occasional extra effort becomes the only way the workload can realistically be completed. Employees stop recording the additional hours because they know overtime will not be approved anyway. The organization quietly benefits from the extra productivity while leadership congratulates teams for maintaining strong output.

The invisible overtime continues.

This arrangement works until it doesn't.

Eventually someone burns out. Someone speaks up. Or someone files a complaint. Suddenly the organization discovers that the off-the-clock work it quietly tolerated now carries serious consequences.

Labor laws exist for a reason. Non-exempt employees must be compensated for the hours they work. When organizations allow unpaid labor to become part of the culture, they expose themselves to legal and financial risk that far outweighs the temporary benefit of increased productivity.

But the legal exposure is only part of the damage.

The larger cost is trust.

Employees quickly recognize the contradiction between leadership's expectations and leadership's policies. They are told to complete more work but also told they cannot be paid for the time required to complete it.

That creates an impossible situation.

Do the work and violate policy or follow the policy and fall behind.

Neither option creates a healthy workplace.

What makes this dynamic particularly dangerous is that many leaders genuinely believe nothing improper is happening. If overtime was not approved, they assume overtime did not occur. If the numbers look strong, they conclude the system must be working.

Meanwhile, the employees carrying the workload know the truth.

Efficiency did not increase.

The hours did.

Shortcuts often produce impressive results in the beginning. Processes move faster. Output increases. Leadership feels validated in its decisions.

But shortcuts rarely remain hidden forever.

Eventually mistakes appear. Compliance issues surface. Employees burn out. Reputation suffers. And the organization begins paying the price for the corners it cut months or even years earlier.

The irony is that most of these problems are entirely avoidable.

Speed itself is not the enemy. Growth is not the enemy. Ambition is not the enemy.

The real danger appears when organizations pursue those goals without maintaining the discipline that protects them.

Strong companies understand that structure, compliance, and thoughtful decision-making are not barriers to success. They are the guardrails that make success sustainable.

Employees notice when leaders respect those guardrails.

They also notice when leaders treat them as optional.

When shortcuts become the norm, the culture slowly shifts. Integrity becomes negotiable. Standards become flexible. And trust begins to erode throughout the organization.

Because once people believe the rules only apply when convenient, those rules stop meaning anything at all.

And when integrity becomes optional, the cost of cutting corners eventually becomes far greater than the time those corners saved.

Chapter 7: Exit Interviews & PIPs: Theater of Lies

If corporate life had a theater department, exit interviews and performance improvement plans would be two of its longest-running productions.

Both are presented as meaningful processes designed to improve the workplace. Both are described as opportunities for communication, feedback, and growth.

And both are often exercises in carefully managed appearances.

Let's start with the exit interview.

In theory, exit interviews exist so organizations can learn why employees leave. Companies say they value honest feedback and want to improve the employee experience. When someone resigns, HR schedules a final meeting to discuss their time with the company and gather insights about what could have been done better.

On paper, it sounds reasonable.

In practice, most employees know the conversation is largely symbolic.

By the time someone reaches the exit interview stage, their decision has already been made. They have accepted another job, submitted their resignation, and mentally moved on. The meeting itself often feels less like a genuine discussion and more like a procedural step that must be completed before their final day.

The questions are predictable.

Why are you leaving?
What did you like about working here?
What could we improve?

Employees quickly learn that answering those questions honestly carries little benefit and some risk. After all, many people leave industries that are surprisingly small. Managers change companies, colleagues cross paths again, and reputations travel farther than expected.

So the answers become polite.

"I found a great opportunity."
"I learned a lot here."
"I wish everyone the best."

Meanwhile, the real reasons often remain unspoken.

The difficult manager.
The impossible workload.
The promotion that went to someone else's friend.
The environment that slowly made coming to work feel exhausting.

HR writes down the polite responses, thanks the employee for their time, and the meeting ends.

The feedback disappears into a database somewhere, rarely connected to the leadership decisions that created the problem in the first place.

The company believes it has gathered useful information.

The departing employee knows nothing will change.

The process is complete.

If exit interviews represent the theater of listening, performance improvement plans represent the theater of fairness.

Few phrases create more anxiety in the workplace than the words "performance improvement plan." Officially known as a PIP, the process is typically described as a structured opportunity for employees to correct performance issues and return to good standing.

In theory, it sounds supportive. A manager identifies concerns, outlines expectations for improvement, and gives the employee time to demonstrate progress.

In reality, many employees already understand what the meeting means the moment they hear those words.

The decision has likely already been made.

As someone who has worked in management, I can say something that many employees quietly suspect: in many organizations, the PIP is not designed to improve performance.

It is designed to create documentation.

Before terminating an employee, companies often need a clear record showing that concerns were addressed and the individual was given an opportunity to improve. The PIP provides that record. It establishes a timeline, defines expectations, and demonstrates that the organization followed a structured process before taking further action.

From a legal standpoint, it makes perfect sense.

From an employee's perspective, it often feels like the beginning of the end.

Most people placed on a PIP quickly realize that the goals outlined in the document are extremely difficult to meet. Expectations may shift, deadlines may be compressed, and the pressure to perform under scrutiny becomes intense.

Even if improvement occurs, the employee knows their reputation inside the organization has likely already been damaged. The PIP becomes a permanent mark that quietly influences future opportunities.

Many employees begin updating their résumés the same day the document is handed to them.

Managers rarely enjoy delivering PIPs either. Despite how the process appears on paper, these conversations are uncomfortable and emotionally draining. Good managers genuinely want their teams to succeed. Sitting across from someone and outlining the steps that could lead to their termination is not a pleasant experience.

But the system demands documentation.

So the process continues.

Forms are completed. Meetings are scheduled. Progress is monitored. Eventually the organization reaches the outcome that was quietly anticipated from the beginning.

The employee leaves.

Leadership then reassures itself that everything was handled professionally and fairly. After all, there was a process. There were meetings. There was documentation.

The system worked exactly as designed.

The deeper problem, however, often remains untouched.

Organizations frequently rely on these formal processes to address individual employees while ignoring the leadership issues that created the situation. A struggling employee might actually be the result of unclear expectations, poor management, or a workload that was never realistic to begin with.

But those problems are far more difficult to document.

So instead, the system focuses on the individual.

One employee leaves. The paperwork is complete. The organization moves forward.

And somewhere else in the company, another employee begins updating their résumé while waiting for their own meeting with HR.

Because when exit interviews and performance improvement plans become the primary tools for addressing workplace issues, the real problems rarely receive the attention they deserve.

The organization congratulates itself for having strong processes.

Meanwhile, employees quietly learn a different lesson.

The outcome may already be decided. The meeting is just part of the script.

Chapter 8: The Meeting That Should Have Been an Email

Most employees have attended at least one meeting that served no meaningful purpose.

Not a quick check-in. Not a collaborative discussion. Not a strategic planning session.

Just a meeting.

A block of time on the calendar where people gather in a conference room or join a video call and quietly wonder why they are there.

Corporate calendars are full of these gatherings. Some exist because someone once decided they were necessary and no one ever revisited the decision. Others appear because leadership believes visibility is the same thing as productivity.

But a special category of meeting exists in many organizations: the meeting that functions primarily as a stage.

I once attended a weekly meeting that perfectly captured this phenomenon.

It lasted an hour.

Attendance was mandatory.

And by the time it ended, everyone in the room understood that the purpose of the meeting had nothing to do with the work we were supposed to be doing.

The meeting opened with management presenting updates about the organization. That part sounded promising. Updates can be helpful. Teams benefit from understanding priorities, upcoming changes, and new initiatives.

But the updates quickly took an unexpected turn.

Instead of discussing projects, processes, or improvements, the conversation shifted toward something else entirely.

Accomplishments.

Specifically, leadership's accomplishments.

For the next hour, employees sat quietly while listening to an extended explanation of how well management was performing. Charts appeared highlighting success. Stories were shared about impressive decisions. Statements were made about the strength of leadership and the remarkable progress the organization was making.

What never appeared in the discussion were the issues employees were actually dealing with.

There was no conversation about improving workflows. No discussion of the problems slowing down productivity. No questions about how teams were managing increasing workloads.

The meeting simply continued, moving from one congratulatory update to another.

Eventually it ended.

Employees returned to their desks and resumed the work they had been pulled away from for an hour.

No decisions had been made. No problems had been solved. No new information had been shared that would help anyone perform their job more effectively.

But leadership had successfully delivered a presentation about leadership.

Meetings like this are surprisingly common.

They exist in organizations that have confused communication with performance. Leaders feel pressure to demonstrate that they are guiding the company forward, and meetings become the easiest way to show that activity is happening.

Unfortunately, activity is not the same thing as progress.

Employees notice the difference immediately.

When meetings become regular events where leadership talks about itself rather than addressing the work that needs to be done, people begin viewing those gatherings as interruptions instead of opportunities.

Productive meetings focus on solving problems. They clarify priorities, remove obstacles, and allow teams to collaborate on decisions that actually move the organization forward.

Performative meetings do the opposite. They consume time without producing outcomes.

Over time, employees learn how to survive them.

They bring laptops and quietly catch up on other tasks while someone speaks. They mute their microphones on video calls and continue working. They listen just enough to know when their name might be mentioned.

In extreme cases, the meeting becomes background noise.

Leadership may still believe they are communicating effectively, but the audience has already disengaged.

The real cost of unnecessary meetings is not just the hour spent sitting in a conference room. It is the cumulative effect of repeatedly interrupting employees who are trying to complete meaningful work.

Consider a simple example. Ten employees attend a one-hour meeting that produces no actionable outcome. That single meeting has consumed ten hours of productive time across the organization.

Now imagine that meeting occurs every week.

The lost productivity quickly becomes staggering.

Ironically, the employees most affected by these meetings are often the ones with the most demanding workloads. They are pulled away from tasks that require concentration in order to attend conversations that contribute nothing to the work itself.

Leadership may believe these gatherings build alignment.

Employees often experience them as delays.

Meetings are not inherently bad. In fact, they are essential when teams need to collaborate, solve problems, or make decisions together.

But good meetings share a few simple characteristics.

They have a clear purpose.

They include only the people necessary to achieve that purpose. And they produce decisions or actions that move the organization forward.

When those elements are missing, the meeting should probably be an email.

Better yet, it may not need to exist at all.

Leaders sometimes forget that the most valuable resource inside any organization is not strategy, technology, or even capital.

It is time.

Every unnecessary meeting spends that resource without asking permission from the people who must give it.

And once employees begin seeing meetings as obstacles instead of tools, leadership has already lost something far more valuable than an hour on the calendar.

They have lost attention.

Chapter 9: HR Isn't Optional

Human Resources occupies a strange position in many organizations.

Ask employees what they think of HR and you will often hear a mix of skepticism and frustration. Ask executives and you may hear something different entirely—references to compliance, risk management, and employee relations.

Both perspectives contain some truth.

In unhealthy organizations, HR often becomes the department everyone loves to blame.

Employees believe HR exists to protect the company instead of helping people. Managers sometimes view HR as an obstacle that slows down decisions. Leadership may treat HR as a necessary administrative function rather than a strategic partner.

When those attitudes take hold, HR becomes marginalized.

Policies are written but not enforced. Concerns are reported but quietly ignored. Managers make decisions without consulting the department responsible for maintaining fairness and consistency across the organization.

Eventually the workplace begins operating without real guardrails.

That is when problems begin multiplying.

Despite the jokes and frustrations that often surround the department, HR serves an essential role in healthy organizations. It provides structure where inconsistency would otherwise thrive. It establishes policies that protect both employees and the company itself.

More importantly, effective HR departments create accountability.

When leadership decisions affect employees' careers, livelihoods, and well-being, someone inside the organization must ensure those decisions are fair, consistent, and legally sound. HR is supposed to provide that oversight.

But oversight only works when leadership allows it.

One of the most common mistakes organizations make is treating HR as an afterthought. Companies invest heavily in sales, operations, and technology while assuming HR can function as a small administrative team quietly handling paperwork in the background.

Then a crisis appears.

A harassment complaint surfaces. A manager crosses a legal line. An employee files a claim the organization never anticipated.

Suddenly leadership realizes the importance of the department they spent years underfunding.

At that point the situation is already far more complicated than it needed to be.

Strong organizations understand that HR is not optional infrastructure. It is part of the leadership framework that protects the company from its own worst instincts.

Without HR involvement, inconsistent management practices begin spreading quickly. One department may enforce policies strictly while another ignores them entirely. One manager treats employees with respect while another operates through intimidation.

Employees quickly recognize these differences.

When policies appear arbitrary or unevenly applied, trust begins to erode.

A well-functioning HR department helps prevent this fragmentation by creating consistency across the organization. Policies are clearly defined. Expectations are communicated. Managers receive guidance on how to address issues before they escalate.

But HR cannot perform this role alone.

The effectiveness of any HR department ultimately depends on the willingness of leadership to listen.

When executives ignore HR advice because it slows down a decision, they are not demonstrating strength. They are removing one of the few systems designed to protect the organization from avoidable mistakes.

Many of the workplace disasters that eventually appear in headlines follow the same pattern. Warning signs were raised early. Concerns were documented. Someone inside the company attempted to address the issue before it became serious.

But leadership decided the warning was inconvenient.

So the warning was ignored.

Weeks or months later, the problem returned with far greater consequences.

Good leaders understand that HR exists to help them avoid exactly those situations.

HR is not supposed to run the company.

But it is supposed to help ensure the company runs responsibly.

When HR is treated as a strategic partner rather than a paperwork department, organizations gain something incredibly valuable: an internal system that reinforces fairness, accountability, and professional standards.

When HR is ignored or sidelined, the organization loses those safeguards.

And once the guardrails disappear, leadership mistakes become far more expensive than anyone expected.

Chapter 10: The Broken Hiring Process

Hiring should be one of the most thoughtful processes inside any organization.

After all, the people a company brings into the business will shape its culture, productivity, and long-term success. A strong hiring process allows organizations to identify capable individuals, evaluate whether they fit the team, and make decisions that strengthen the company over time.

At least, that is how hiring is supposed to work.

In reality, many hiring processes have become chaotic, inefficient, and strangely disconnected from the actual work the position requires. Candidates often find themselves navigating a system that seems less designed to identify talent and more designed to exhaust it.

Job descriptions frequently read like wish lists created by committee. Employers ask for five years of experience in technologies that have only existed for three. They search for candidates who possess every possible skill while offering compensation that suggests the role is entry level.

The mythical "perfect candidate" becomes the standard.

Meanwhile, qualified people who could easily perform the job are screened out by automated systems long before a human ever sees their résumé.

This is often the first breakdown in the hiring process: organizations have handed the earliest stage of candidate evaluation to software that filters applicants based on keyword matches rather than real capability.

Resumes disappear into digital systems that quietly reject candidates who might have brought valuable skills and perspectives to the company.

But even candidates who successfully navigate the initial screening often encounter another obstacle: the endless interview cycle.

It is not uncommon for applicants to go through three, four, or even six rounds of interviews. Each conversation introduces them to another manager, another executive, or another team member who needs to provide input on the decision.

Weeks pass. Sometimes months.

Candidates prepare, schedule time away from their current jobs, and invest significant energy in demonstrating their qualifications. Throughout the process they are told the organization is excited about their potential and eager to move forward.

Then the communication stops.

Emails go unanswered. Updates never arrive. The candidate is left wondering whether the role still exists or whether the company simply lost interest.

This phenomenon—commonly referred to as ghosting—has become one of the most frustrating aspects of the modern hiring process.

Ironically, many of the organizations that complain about a shortage of talent are the same ones quietly losing strong candidates through disorganized hiring practices.

The problem does not end once someone is hired.

In many cases, the role the employee begins performing looks very different from the job that was advertised. Responsibilities expand, expectations shift, and the support systems that were described during interviews never fully materialize.

Employees quickly realize the position they accepted was only partially defined when they agreed to take it.

In fast-moving industries, hiring dysfunction can become even more pronounced during market swings. During boom periods, companies rush to expand teams as quickly as possible. Hiring standards become flexible because leadership wants to capture as much opportunity as the market offers.

When conditions change, those same organizations suddenly freeze hiring entirely.

Departments that were recently expanding are now struggling to maintain operations with shrinking staff. Managers are forced to stretch existing employees across multiple roles while leadership debates when—or whether—new hiring will be approved again.

Employees experience these cycles as instability.

Candidates experience them as confusion.

Organizations experience them as a persistent struggle to find the right people.

But the truth is that many companies are not failing to find talent. They are failing to manage the systems that identify and recruit it.

Strong hiring processes share a few common characteristics.

They define the role clearly.

They focus on the skills that actually matter for the work being performed.

They respect the candidate's time by moving efficiently through the process.

And they communicate honestly about expectations on both sides.

When those elements are missing, hiring becomes unpredictable and frustrating for everyone involved.

Candidates feel undervalued. Hiring managers feel overwhelmed. Teams remain understaffed while the search for the mythical perfect hire continues.

Eventually organizations begin wondering why it has become so difficult to attract strong employees.

The answer is often simpler than they expect.

People want to work for organizations that demonstrate competence before they ever walk through the door.

And the hiring process is the first opportunity a company has to prove it.

When that process appears disorganized, slow, or disconnected from reality, candidates receive a message long before their first day of work.

If the hiring process is this chaotic, what will the rest of the organization look like?

Chapter 11: Why Working for a Family-Run Company Is a Terrible Idea

Family businesses often present themselves as something special.

During interviews, candidates are told the company operates differently from large corporations. Leadership emphasizes the close-knit environment, the personal relationships, and the sense of loyalty that comes from working for a family-run organization.

"We treat everyone like family here."

To someone looking for stability and community, that message can sound appealing.

But experienced employees often hear something very different.

They hear a warning.

Family-run companies can absolutely succeed, and many of them do. Some of the most respected organizations in the world began as family enterprises and continue operating that way today. When those companies are managed well, family leadership can create strong values and long-term vision.

Unfortunately, that is not always how things unfold.

In many cases, family-run companies struggle with a problem that professional organizations work hard to avoid: the absence of objective leadership.

When ownership and management are tightly intertwined with family relationships, business decisions often become influenced by personal dynamics rather than professional judgment.

Employees quickly discover that the organizational chart does not tell the whole story.

The real hierarchy exists somewhere else.

It may exist around the dinner table during holidays. It may exist in conversations between siblings who hold unofficial influence. It may exist in long-standing relationships that predate the company itself.

But wherever it exists, employees eventually learn the same lesson.

They are not part of the inner circle.

That realization becomes especially clear when promotions, leadership roles, and strategic decisions begin appearing within the family network.

A new executive suddenly appears in the leadership team.

The résumé may be thin, but the last name looks familiar.

Employees who have spent years building experience within the organization watch as leadership roles are filled by relatives who bypass the usual expectations of performance and qualification.

When questions arise, the explanation is often vague.

"They understand the vision."
"They've been around the business for years."
"They know the culture."

What those phrases usually mean is much simpler.

They're family.

Once employees recognize that family relationships influence leadership decisions, the workplace begins to change in subtle ways.

Feedback becomes risky. Employees hesitate to raise concerns about management decisions if those decisions involve someone related to ownership. Performance standards may appear uneven depending on who holds the role.

In some situations, conflicts that would normally be addressed through professional channels become complicated by family loyalty.

Managers may find themselves unable to discipline underperforming employees because those employees share the same last name as the person who signs their paycheck.

Accountability begins to fade.

The problem becomes even more visible during moments of disagreement. In professionally managed organizations, conflicts about strategy or performance are usually resolved through structured decision-making processes.

In family-run companies, those disagreements can quickly become personal.

Employees may find themselves navigating disputes that have less to do with business strategy and more to do with family dynamics that existed long before the company was founded.

What looks like a leadership debate from the outside may actually be a continuation of a sibling rivalry that began decades earlier.

Employees caught in the middle often feel powerless to address the situation.

Another challenge appears when organizations try to grow beyond their original structure. As companies expand, leadership responsibilities become more complex. Managing larger teams, navigating regulatory environments, and scaling operations require increasingly sophisticated leadership skills.

Family loyalty alone cannot meet those demands.

But bringing in outside leadership can feel threatening to family members who have always held authority within the business. As a result, companies sometimes resist adding experienced professionals to the leadership team.

Instead, the same group of individuals continues managing a much larger organization than they were originally prepared to lead.

Employees notice the strain.

Decisions slow down. Internal politics increase. Talented professionals who hoped to build careers within the company eventually recognize that advancement opportunities are limited.

After all, certain roles may already be reserved for someone whose future leadership position was decided years ago.

This does not mean every family-run business is dysfunctional. Many operate successfully for generations because family leaders understand the importance of professionalism and accountability.

The difference is that strong family-run companies establish clear boundaries between family relationships and business operations.

Leadership roles are earned rather than inherited. Outside professionals are welcomed rather than viewed as threats. Accountability applies to everyone, including family members.

Unfortunately, not every organization reaches that level of maturity.

When family loyalty consistently outweighs professional judgment, employees eventually face a difficult choice.

They can continue navigating a system where advancement depends on relationships they will never have.

Or they can find an organization where performance matters more than last names.

For many talented professionals, the decision becomes obvious.

Because once employees realize that leadership opportunities are determined at the family dinner table instead of the conference table, the future of their career becomes much easier to predict.

And not in a good way.

Chapter 12: "We're a Family" and Other Corporate Lies

Few phrases in corporate life make me cringe harder than: "We're a family." No. You are not my family (*I'll say it louder for the people in the back*). You are my employer.

And that's okay. Employment isn't love, it's an agreement. The healthiest companies remember that boundaries build trust.

Families don't hand out performance improvement plans. Families don't ghost you after three interviews. Families don't fire people because quarterly profits dipped. And families sure as hell don't expect you to sacrifice nights, weekends, and sanity in exchange for pizza Fridays.

And let's be honest, even real families aren't exactly the gold standard. Families argue at Thanksgiving, hold grudges for decades, and fight over who gets Grandma's china. So if your company culture is modeled after "family"? You're already in trouble.

The "we're a family" line is one of the oldest manipulation tactics in corporate history. Leaders trot it out whenever they need employees to do more for less. And employees know it. The second those words hit the air, the eye rolls begin.

Here's when you'll usually hear it:

- **Right before layoffs.**
  "We're a family, and sometimes families have to make tough choices."
  Translation: *Pack your desk.*

- **When overtime becomes mandatory.**
  "We're a family, and families pitch in."
  Translation: *Cancel your weekend plans.*
- **When employee surveys tank.**
  "We're a family, and families don't always get along."
  Translation: *Stop complaining; you're making leadership look bad.*

And the hypocrisy doesn't stop there. I once applied for a job at a company that made every applicant take a personality test. The president actually called me to review my results — like I was waiting on lab work. He wanted to make sure I'd "fit in with the office dynamic," especially with his wife, who just so happened to be the office manager. He wanted to ensure the "family harmony" stayed intact.

Let's unpack that. You're not hiring based on skills or qualifications. Hiring for harmony instead of honesty is how cultures turn cultish. That's not community; that's control with coffee mugs.

Companies don't need to play the family card to build loyalty. They just need to be professional. Pay people fairly. Apply policies consistently. Respect boundaries. Communicate honestly. Support growth. That's it. No gimmicks required.

Executives, let me spell it out: stop calling your company a family. You're not fooling anyone. Every time you say it, employees start updating their résumés.

If you want loyalty, drop the manipulation and deliver fairness. Because every time you call your company a family, you remind employees it isn't —and the more you say it, the faster they look for the exit. Real belonging isn't declared; it's demonstrated, one fair decision at a time.

Chapter 13: The Myth of Meritocracy

Ask most organizations how promotions are determined and the answer usually sounds reassuring.

Leaders talk about performance. They talk about dedication, measurable results, and the value of rewarding employees who contribute the most to the company's success. Job postings describe career paths where strong work and consistent effort lead naturally to advancement.

It is a comforting narrative.

Work hard. Perform well. Earn the next opportunity.

But inside many workplaces, employees gradually learn that the system works differently.

Performance certainly matters, but it is rarely the only factor shaping someone's career. In practice, promotions often depend on something far less predictable: relationships with leadership.

Who trusts you.
Who advocates for you.
Who likes working with you.
And sometimes, who you have unintentionally upset along the way.

This reality can feel uncomfortable to acknowledge because it challenges the belief that workplaces operate as pure meritocracies. Most employees want to believe their efforts will be evaluated fairly and objectively. They want to believe the quality of their work speaks for itself.

Unfortunately, organizations are still run by human beings, and human beings bring their own perceptions, biases, and personal dynamics into every decision.

A talented employee who builds strong relationships with leadership may receive opportunities earlier than others. Another employee with equally strong technical skills may struggle to gain visibility simply because their work happens behind the scenes.

And occasionally, someone who challenges established practices may find themselves in a far more complicated position.

Organizations often say they value people who speak up and raise concerns. In theory, constructive criticism helps companies improve their systems and avoid mistakes. Leaders encourage employees to bring forward ideas that strengthen the business.

But that encouragement can have limits.

Calling attention to uncomfortable truths—especially in industries where certain practices have become normalized—can make people uneasy. When those concerns challenge influential individuals or established methods, the person raising them may quietly develop a reputation for being "difficult."

Sometimes the label appears subtly.

"He's very strong technically, but not always easy to work with."
"She asks a lot of questions."
"They don't always align with leadership."

These descriptions may sound mild on the surface, but they can quietly influence career trajectories.

In industries where professional networks are tightly connected, reputations travel quickly. A single disagreement with the wrong person can ripple far beyond one workplace. People move between companies, carry impressions with them, and share opinions about colleagues long after the original situation has passed.

In those environments, relationships become even more powerful.

A strong professional network can open doors that might otherwise remain closed. At the same time, strained relationships with influential figures can make career progression unexpectedly difficult—even for people who consistently deliver high-quality work.

For employees who value integrity and transparency, this dynamic can be especially frustrating. They may believe that pointing out problems or challenging questionable practices will strengthen the organization. Sometimes it does.

Other times, the reaction is less constructive.

Instead of addressing the issue being raised, leadership may begin focusing on the person who raised it. The conversation shifts from the substance of the concern to the tone of the individual delivering it.

Eventually the message becomes clear.

Performance alone is not enough.

Understanding the importance of relationships does not mean abandoning professionalism or integrity. Healthy organizations still need employees who ask difficult questions and identify problems before they grow larger.

But it does mean recognizing that workplaces are complex social systems as well as professional ones. Leadership decisions are influenced by trust, perception, and personal dynamics in addition to measurable results.

Employees who navigate those realities effectively often combine strong performance with strong relationships. They build credibility not only through the quality of their work but also through communication, collaboration, and the trust they develop with the people around them.

When organizations manage this balance well, merit and relationships reinforce each other.

When they manage it poorly, the result is a workplace where advancement feels arbitrary and unpredictable.

Employees begin watching who receives opportunities rather than how those opportunities are earned. Over time, that observation shapes how people approach their work. Some become disengaged. Others focus more energy on office politics than on improving the business itself.

And once that shift occurs, the organization begins drifting away from the meritocratic ideal it originally promised.

True meritocracies are rare because they require constant effort to maintain. Leaders must actively challenge their own biases, evaluate performance honestly, and ensure opportunities are distributed based on genuine contribution rather than personal comfort.

That level of discipline is difficult.

But without it, the system quietly evolves into something else.

A workplace where relationships determine opportunity, performance becomes secondary, and employees slowly realize that the path forward depends less on what they accomplish and more on who happens to be standing beside them.

Chapter 14: What Real Leadership Actually Looks Like

After spending time examining broken leadership systems, it would be easy to conclude that effective leadership is rare or unrealistic.

It isn't.

Strong leadership exists in organizations of every size. It appears in companies that operate quietly without fanfare, often far from the spotlight of business media or leadership conferences. These organizations rarely produce viral LinkedIn posts or bestselling leadership memoirs.

They simply function well.

Their employees understand what is expected of them. Problems are addressed before they become crises. Decisions are made with clarity rather than confusion.

And most importantly, the people inside those organizations trust their leadership.

The difference between effective leadership and dysfunctional leadership is not complicated. It does not require elaborate management theories or carefully constructed corporate philosophies.

It begins with something much simpler.

Responsibility.

Real leaders understand that leadership is not a privilege. It is an obligation. The moment someone accepts authority over others, they also accept responsibility for the environment those people work within.

That responsibility begins with honesty.

Employees can handle difficult news. Markets fluctuate, companies struggle, and strategies sometimes fail. What employees struggle with is leadership that refuses to acknowledge reality. When problems are hidden behind corporate language or optimistic messaging, trust begins to erode.

Strong leaders tell the truth about the challenges their organizations face. They explain what is happening, why it is happening, and what the organization plans to do about it.

Transparency creates alignment.

Another defining characteristic of strong leadership is consistency.

In dysfunctional workplaces, policies are often applied unevenly. Certain individuals receive flexibility while others face strict expectations. Over time, this inconsistency destroys morale because employees begin to realize the rules are not the same for everyone.

Effective leaders eliminate this uncertainty by applying standards evenly. Expectations are clear, and accountability does not depend on someone's position or personal relationship with leadership.

Fairness becomes visible.

Real leaders also understand that their job is not to control every aspect of the organization's work.

Their job is to create the conditions where capable people can succeed.

That begins with hiring the right individuals and trusting them to perform their responsibilities. Micromanagement often appears when leaders lack confidence in their teams or lack clarity about their own priorities. Instead of guiding the organization strategically, they become trapped in operational details.

Strong leaders resist that instinct.

They focus on removing obstacles rather than creating them.

When teams encounter challenges, effective leaders step in to provide resources, clarify priorities, or adjust expectations. They do not respond by assigning blame or increasing pressure without addressing the underlying problem.

This approach creates something incredibly valuable inside an organization: psychological safety.

Employees who feel safe raising concerns are far more likely to identify problems early. They speak openly about inefficiencies, potential risks, and opportunities for improvement.

In unhealthy environments, employees often stay silent because they believe speaking up will damage their reputation or threaten their job.

In healthy organizations, leaders actively encourage those conversations.

They understand that the most dangerous problems are often the ones nobody feels comfortable discussing.

Another trait that separates strong leaders from ineffective ones is humility.

Leadership roles can easily create the illusion that authority equals expertise. Some leaders begin believing that their position automatically makes them the smartest person in the room.

The best leaders know that assumption is dangerous.

They surround themselves with capable people and actively seek input from individuals who understand the day-to-day realities of the organization. Frontline employees frequently see operational problems long before executives do.

Effective leaders listen to those perspectives rather than dismissing them.

Listening, in fact, may be one of the most underrated leadership skills.

Finally, strong leaders understand something that many organizations forget: leadership is not about personal recognition.

It is about stewardship.

The leader's job is to protect the organization's mission, support the people responsible for carrying it out, and ensure that decisions are made responsibly.

When teams succeed, strong leaders credit the people who did the work.

When problems occur, they take responsibility for solving them.

Employees notice this difference immediately.

They can tell when leadership exists primarily to promote itself. They can also tell when leadership exists to support the organization.

One approach creates distance.

The other creates loyalty.

Ultimately, effective leadership does not require extraordinary charisma or elaborate strategies.

It requires discipline.

Tell the truth.

Apply standards fairly.

Hire capable people and trust them to do their jobs.

Listen to the individuals closest to the work.

And accept responsibility for the outcomes.

These principles are simple.

Practicing them consistently, however, requires something many organizations struggle with.

Courage.

Because real leadership means making decisions that are sometimes uncomfortable. It means addressing problems early instead of ignoring them until they become crises. It means holding people accountable even when those people are influential or politically connected.

Organizations that embrace these principles rarely appear chaotic or dramatic from the outside. Their workplaces are stable. Their teams understand their goals. Their employees believe their efforts matter.

Trust becomes part of the culture.

And once trust exists, many of the problems discussed earlier in this book begin to disappear naturally.

Because healthy cultures are not built through slogans or motivational campaigns.

They are built by leaders who understand their responsibility and take it seriously.

In other words, leaders who decide to do something remarkably simple.

They decide to do better.

Chapter 15: How Leaders Accidently Create Toxic Cultures

Very few organizations set out to create toxic workplaces.

No executive gathers their leadership team and announces that the company's goal for the year is to build an environment filled with distrust, resentment, and frustration. Most leaders genuinely believe they are trying to build successful organizations where employees can do meaningful work.

And yet toxic cultures appear everywhere.

They appear in companies that once had strong reputations. They appear in organizations that proudly display their mission statements on the walls. They even appear in businesses led by people who consider themselves thoughtful and ethical.

Toxic cultures rarely emerge from a single catastrophic decision.

Instead, they develop gradually through a series of small choices about what leadership is willing to tolerate.

One of the most common examples involves the high-performing employee who treats everyone around them poorly.

Every organization has encountered this situation at some point. A particular employee generates impressive numbers, closes large deals, or produces results that appear valuable to the company. On paper, they are a top performer.

But behind the scenes, their behavior creates serious problems.

They belittle coworkers. They refuse to collaborate. They create unnecessary conflict with other teams. Sometimes they treat junior employees in ways that would never be acceptable if anyone else behaved the same way.

Leadership notices the behavior, but addressing it feels complicated.

After all, the individual is producing results.

So the organization makes a quiet compromise.

The behavior is tolerated.

At first the justification seems reasonable. Leaders tell themselves the situation will improve over time. They convince themselves the employee simply has a strong personality or an intense work style.

But the rest of the organization sees something very different.

They see that performance excuses behavior.

Once that message spreads, the culture begins shifting quickly.

Employees start understanding that certain individuals operate under a different set of rules. Respect, collaboration, and professionalism become optional if someone generates enough revenue or holds enough influence.

The damage does not stop with that one employee.

Other team members begin adjusting their behavior to match the environment they see around them. Some employees disengage, deciding that professionalism is not valued anyway. Others attempt to mimic the aggressive behavior that leadership appears to reward.

In either case, the culture deteriorates.

Another common source of toxicity emerges when organizations ignore bullying managers.

Unlike the high-performing employee who mistreats coworkers, these individuals often hold leadership positions themselves. Their behavior may appear as constant criticism, public humiliation, or intimidation disguised as accountability.

Employees working under these managers experience daily stress. They hesitate to raise concerns because previous attempts resulted in retaliation or dismissal.

Eventually someone reports the behavior.

Leadership listens, thanks the employee for speaking up, and promises to review the situation.

Then nothing happens.

The manager remains in place. The behavior continues. And employees quietly learn that reporting problems does not lead to meaningful change.

In many cases leadership avoids confronting the issue because the manager produces results or because addressing the behavior would require uncomfortable conversations.

But the cost of that avoidance is enormous.

When employees believe bullying behavior will be tolerated, trust in leadership begins to collapse.

Favoritism creates another pathway toward toxic cultures.

In workplaces where certain employees receive special treatment based on personal relationships with leadership, the perception of fairness disappears quickly. Promotions appear predetermined. Opportunities seem to circulate among the same group of individuals.

Employees outside that circle begin asking themselves why they should continue investing effort when advancement feels impossible.

Over time, frustration turns into disengagement.

The final ingredient in many toxic cultures is leadership's refusal to address obvious problems.

In every organization there are moments when a problem becomes visible to nearly everyone involved. Workflows break down. Teams struggle with unrealistic workloads. Communication between departments collapses.

Employees discuss the issue constantly.

Leadership, however, often responds with silence.

Sometimes the problem feels too complicated to address quickly. Sometimes acknowledging it would require admitting that earlier decisions were mistakes. And sometimes leaders simply hope the situation will resolve itself without requiring intervention.

But problems rarely solve themselves.

When leadership refuses to confront obvious issues, employees draw their own conclusions. They begin assuming that leadership either does not understand what is happening inside the organization or does not care enough to fix it.

Neither conclusion inspires confidence.

Eventually the workplace environment begins reflecting those assumptions. Collaboration declines. Employees stop volunteering ideas because they believe nothing will change anyway.

In extreme cases, the most capable employees quietly begin searching for opportunities elsewhere.

Leadership often expresses surprise when this happens.

They review exit interviews and discover that employees describe the environment as toxic. Managers wonder how the culture deteriorated so quickly.

The truth is that the culture did not change overnight. It evolved gradually through a series of tolerated behaviors.

The high performer who mistreated coworkers.

The bullying manager who remained in power.

The favoritism that influenced promotions.

The problems everyone could see but nobody addressed.

Each of these decisions sent a message to the organization. Individually, those messages may have seemed minor. Together, they created the culture.

The lesson for leaders is simple but uncomfortable. Toxic cultures are rarely the result of intentional decisions. They are the result of tolerated ones.

Every behavior leadership allows to continue becomes part of the organization's culture. Every problem that goes unaddressed teaches employees what standards actually exist inside the company.

Culture is not defined by mission statements or motivational posters.

It is defined by the behavior leaders choose to allow.

When leaders tolerate disrespect, the culture becomes disrespectful.

When leaders tolerate favoritism, the culture becomes political.

When leaders tolerate obvious problems, the culture becomes cynical.

But when leaders choose accountability instead of convenience, something different happens. The culture improves. Not because leadership demanded it, but because leadership demonstrated it.

And employees are always paying attention to what leadership chooses to tolerate.

Chapter 16: Burnout Isn't Laziness

Few words are misunderstood in the modern workplace quite like the word *burnout*.

When employees begin showing signs of exhaustion, disengagement, or declining productivity, the conversation often turns quickly toward motivation. Managers wonder whether the employee has lost their work ethic. Leaders question whether people are simply less resilient than they once were.

In the worst cases, burnout becomes shorthand for laziness.

But burnout has very little to do with laziness.

In fact, it most often appears in the exact opposite group of people— the ones who cared the most about doing their jobs well.

Burnout rarely arrives overnight. It develops slowly, often beginning in environments where employees are trying to succeed despite systems that make success unnecessarily difficult.

At first the signs are subtle.

Employees begin working longer hours to keep up with growing expectations. They take on additional responsibilities when teams shrink or workloads increase. They try to solve problems that leadership has not addressed because someone still has to keep the work moving forward.

For a while, this effort feels productive. Dedicated employees convince themselves they are simply stepping up during a challenging period.

But when the pressure never eases, something begins to change.

The extra effort stops feeling temporary.

It becomes permanent.

Employees who once took pride in their work begin realizing that the problems surrounding them are not being solved. Meetings continue without producing decisions. Hiring delays leave teams understaffed. Leadership promises improvements that never quite arrive.

Eventually people begin asking themselves a difficult question.

Is anything actually going to change?

When the answer appears to be no, motivation begins to fade.

Burnout does not begin when someone stops caring.

It begins when someone realizes that caring no longer makes a difference.

This moment is often misunderstood by leadership. Managers may notice that a once highly engaged employee has become quieter. The person who used to volunteer ideas during meetings now listens without speaking. Tasks that were once completed with enthusiasm are now approached with visible fatigue.

From the outside, it may appear as though the employee has lost interest in their job.

From the inside, something else has happened.

The employee has simply reached the point where constant effort no longer feels worthwhile.

Many burned-out employees continue performing their responsibilities at a professional level. They show up, complete their assignments, and meet the expectations required to keep their role.

What disappears is the extra energy.

The initiative.

The willingness to go beyond what is required.

These employees are not lazy. They are tired.

Tired of navigating systems that seem designed to create obstacles rather than remove them. Tired of watching capable colleagues leave while workloads increase for those who remain. Tired of hearing about improvements that never seem to materialize.

Over time, burnout spreads quietly through organizations.

One employee disengages. Then another. Teams that once collaborated enthusiastically begin operating on autopilot. Work still gets done, but the sense of purpose that once energized the environment slowly fades.

Leadership sometimes responds to this shift by increasing pressure.

More meetings.

More performance metrics.

More reminders about expectations.

Unfortunately, pressure rarely fixes burnout. It usually accelerates it.

Burnout is not a productivity problem. It is a leadership signal.

It tells an organization that the systems surrounding employees are no longer sustainable. It signals that workloads, expectations, and support structures have fallen out of balance.

When leaders recognize burnout as a warning sign, they have an opportunity to repair the environment that created it.

When leaders misinterpret burnout as laziness, they often double down on the very behaviors that caused the problem in the first place.

The result is predictable.

More employees begin looking for ways out.

And once a workplace reaches the point where its most capable people are quietly planning their exit, the organization has already lost something far more valuable than productivity.

It has lost belief.

Employees stop believing that leadership will fix the problems they see every day. They stop believing their extra effort will create meaningful change.

And when belief disappears, even the most talented workforce eventually begins running on empty.

Burnout is not laziness.

It is what happens when dedicated people spend too long trying to succeed inside broken systems.

Chapter 17: Accountability for All

If there's one thing employees sniff out faster than bad coffee, it's a double standard. Nothing destroys morale faster than watching leaders skate by without consequences while everyone else gets written up for breathing too loudly

Accountability is supposed to be the backbone of a healthy workplace. But in too many companies, it's selective. Rules apply to some. Favorites, executives, or top performers? Exempt. That's not culture. That's hypocrisy in business casual.

I once worked with an employee who was exceptional—smart, reliable, the kind of person who made everyone else's job easier. One day, they made a judgment call to help a customer. It wasn't reckless; it was reasonable. But because the situation went sideways, they were disciplined. Meanwhile, the manager who created the mess? Not even a conversation.

That wasn't accountability. That was scapegoating.

Accountability without fairness is just theater, and everyone in the audience knows who the understudy will be next time.

And employees notice.

They always notice.

Selective accountability breeds resentment. When people see that leaders get a pass, they stop trying. They stop trusting. And eventually, they stop staying.

This happens everywhere. Executives bend policies, sales teams break promises, or a "rainmaker" gets away with treating coworkers like dirt because they bring in revenue.

The message is clear: results matter more than respect.

And once employees understand that, the consequences show up quickly.

- **Resentment.** People don't respect leaders who preach integrity but practice favoritism.
- **Disengagement.** Why put in effort if the game is rigged?
- **Turnover.** Your best employees will walk, and the ones who stay will do the bare minimum for survival.

And don't even get me started on recognition. The same handful of people win every "President's Club" trip while the people quietly holding everything together get a mug and a leftover cupcake.

When reward and punishment have nothing to do with fairness, your culture starts to rot from the inside out.

Executives, let's make this simple: Accountability that skips the powerful isn't accountability; it's performance art. If the CEO's kid misses deadlines, they face the same consequences as the intern. If a top performer crosses a line, you deal with it instead of hiding behind their numbers. If a manager mistreats people, you don't "reassign" them; you remove them.

Because the second employees see leadership protecting bad behavior, credibility dies. And once credibility dies, culture follows. Fairness isn't optional. Consistency isn't optional. Accountability isn't optional. Employees see everything. They talk about it in group chats, at lunch, and in job interviews somewhere else. You may think you're keeping secrets. You're not.

So if you truly want loyalty, start by holding everyone—***everyone***—to the same standard. Because when accountability is real, trust is automatic. And when trust is gone, no amount of swag or slogans will save you.

Leadership rarely loses trust in one dramatic moment. It disappears slowly, drip by drip, every time fairness takes a back seat.

Chapter 18: Stop Yelling at the People

Every workplace has its cast of characters.

Some make the day survivable. They share a laugh, pitch in when things go sideways, and keep the wheels from flying off.

Others do the opposite. They yell. They blame. They turn ordinary problems into personal attacks and somehow still call it "leadership."

You've probably met a few of them.

• **The Screamer.** Thinks volume equals authority. Raises their voice whenever someone disagrees, as if intimidation were a management style.

• **The Blamer.** Nothing is ever their fault. Deadlines missed? Someone else dropped the ball. Budget overrun? Must've been accounting. They could spill coffee on their own laptop and still blame IT.

• **The Drama King or Queen.** Every hiccup is a catastrophe. Every email is urgent. They thrive on chaos because without it, they'd have to do actual work.

• **The Martyr.** Constant sighing. Loud groaning. Public reminders about how overworked they are. The goal isn't solving problems — it's collecting sympathy.

• **The Passive-Aggressive Pro.** Won't yell outright, but will cc your boss on every email, make snide comments in meetings, and "forget" to share important information.

Honestly, just yell. It's less exhausting.

These people exist in almost every workplace. But the real problem isn't that they exist.

The real problem is that leadership lets them stay.

The number of times I've heard, "Oh, that's just how they are," is mind-numbing. Really?

Then they can "just" go work somewhere else. Because every time leadership protects a toxic employee, it sends a message to the entire team: Bad behavior is acceptable — as long as it comes from the right person.

And somehow this behavior keeps getting rewarded.

Loud, abrasive employees get labeled **"passionate."**

Managers who scream are called **"intense."**

People who humiliate coworkers are described as **"direct."**

Let's call it what it actually is. Bullying in business attire.

Here's the reality most leaders forget: nobody succeeds alone.

Every project, every sale, every system — all of it depends on teams. Tear one person down and the entire structure weakens.

Screaming at people doesn't improve the work. It just makes people dread coming to work.

And leaders, if you allow it, you're part of the problem. Every time you excuse it, you teach everyone watching that respect is optional.

Respect isn't earned by volume.

It's earned by example.

If you have to raise your voice to be heard, you've already lost the room.

Culture isn't defined by what you say during an all-hands meeting. It's defined by what you tolerate at 3 p.m. on a Tuesday when someone loses their temper.

If the people generating the most revenue are also generating the most fear, you don't have a performance problem.

You have a credibility problem.

I'm the nicest person you'll ever meet — until someone starts yelling at me.

I'll move mountains for you. I'll help solve problems. I'll stay late if the team needs it.

But the second the shouting starts, I'm done.

Because yelling isn't passion. It's immaturity with a volume knob.

So let's simplify this.

Stop yelling at people.

Stop cursing at coworkers who are trying to do their jobs.

Stop hiding behind "stress" as an excuse for bad behavior.

Start acting like adults who respect the humans around them.

Kindness doesn't weaken authority. It strengthens it.

Be kind. Or be gone.

Chapter 19: Plain Talk, Real Trust

If there's one thing that erodes trust faster than a bad decision, it's corporate spin.

Employees can forgive mistakes. What they won't forgive is being treated like they're stupid. And nothing screams "we think you're dumb" louder than jargon-filled announcements that avoid the truth.

I've sat through meetings where "strategic realignment," "operational optimization," and "paradigm shift" were tossed around so much I wasn't sure if I was in a business meeting or a TED Talk about word salad. If communication requires a decoder ring, you're not being strategic; you're being unclear.

By the end, nobody had a clue what was actually happening. But leadership? They left high-fiving, convinced they'd nailed it. That wasn't communication. It was improv theater with bad lighting.

Here's what employees actually want from leaders:

1. What's happening.
2. Why it's happening.
3. How it affects them.

That's it. No motivational monologues. No buzzword gymnastics. Just the truth in plain English.

But too many leaders hide behind corporate poetry. Layoffs become "right-sizing." Fines become "compliance enhancements." Panic becomes "strategic agility." And employees? They see right through it.

People aren't rolling their eyes because of the bad news. They're rolling their eyes because of how badly it's delivered.

Here's a secret every executive should write on a sticky note: **Employees already know.** They know when the numbers are bad. They know when layoffs are coming. They know when the "urgent company-wide meeting" on Friday afternoon is going to be rough.

So stop pretending they don't. By the time leadership crafts its perfect email about "operational restructuring," employees are already texting each other translations like: "We're screwed." And they're usually right.

Many moons ago, worked for a company that refused to say the word "layoff." Instead, they'd say things like, "We're adjusting capacity to align with market realities." By the third "adjustment," people weren't even pretending to believe it. Morale tanked faster than the company stock.

Executives, honesty doesn't erode credibility, it enhances it. Plain talk isn't weakness; it's strength. It's credibility. People don't expect perfection, but they do expect honesty. If you tell the truth, even when it's uncomfortable, you earn trust. If you spin, even when it's minor, you lose it.

So say it straight: "We overhired." "We made mistakes." "Here's what we're doing to fix it."

That's leadership.

Because clarity doesn't make bad news worse, but it makes it bearable. Trust isn't built through slogans; it's built through honest, clear words and sentences that actually mean something.

If your employees leave a meeting with more questions than answers, you didn't communicate; you performed.

Drop the theater.

Drop the jargon.

Talk like a human.

Because in the end, plain talk builds real trust — and real trust is the only thing that keeps people from quietly updating their résumés while you're still on stage.

Chapter 20: A CEO's Guide to Fixing Dysfunction

Let's cut the excuses.

If your company feels chaotic, it's not because "people don't want to work anymore." It's because leadership allowed confusion, favoritism, and dysfunction to replace clarity, fairness, and accountability.

Leadership problems rarely start in the field.

They start in the mirror.

The good news is that dysfunction isn't permanent. Companies don't have to run like circuses. A workplace can actually function well. People can trust leadership. Teams can succeed without constant chaos.

But it requires executives to stop performing leadership and start practicing it.

And that means doing the unglamorous work that actually fixes things.

Here's the playbook.

1. Respect your people.

Not just the top performers. Not just the loudest voices in the room. Everyone.

Respect means fair pay, clear expectations, and trusting employees to do their jobs without a babysitter hovering over every decision. If you treat adults like children, don't act surprised when they start acting like teenagers.

Respect isn't complicated. It's just rare.

2. Choose leaders wisely.

Stop promoting people because they've been around the longest. Stop rewarding connections, friendships, or family ties with management roles.

Leadership isn't a prize for tenure.

If someone doesn't like working with people, they shouldn't manage them. If someone thinks intimidation equals authority, they shouldn't be anywhere near a leadership title.

Leadership is responsibility. Treat it like one.

3. Hold everyone accountable.

Accountability that skips the executive floor isn't accountability.

If the rules don't apply to everyone, they don't mean anything. Employees know exactly when favoritism is happening, and once they see it, trust evaporates fast.

If a top performer crosses the line, deal with it. If a manager mistreats their team, address it. If leadership breaks the rules, fix it publicly.

Standards only matter when they apply to everyone in the building.

4. Simplify communication.

Stop calling chaos a "strategic pivot."

Stop calling layoffs "right-sizing."

Stop dressing up mistakes as "learning opportunities."

Speak like a human being. Tell people what's happening, why it's happening, and how it affects them. That's it.

Employees can handle the truth.

What they can't handle is spin.

5. Invest in real HR.

HR is not the party planning committee. It's not the department that orders cupcakes and schedules morale surveys.

Good HR protects your people and your company at the same time.

Strong HR departments enforce standards, address problems early, and keep leadership from making avoidable mistakes. Weak HR departments quietly collect paperwork while dysfunction spreads.

If your HR team doesn't have real authority, you don't have HR.

You have administrative assistants with better titles.

6. Listen where the truth lives.

If you want to understand what's really happening inside your company, stop relying only on polished executive reports.

Talk to the people doing the work.

Talk to the analyst juggling three projects.
The customer service rep handling angry calls.
The coordinator who hasn't taken a lunch break in two years.

They know where the systems are broken. They know where the delays happen. They know which decisions are making their jobs harder.

And if you actually listen, they'll tell you.

7. Prioritize ethics over ego.

Every company faces moments where cutting corners looks tempting.

Maybe a deal could close faster if someone ignores a warning sign. Maybe a top producer should get a pass because their numbers look great. Maybe addressing a leadership problem would create too much internal conflict.

Those moments define a company.

The second integrity becomes optional, the countdown to bigger problems begins.

Ethics aren't a "nice to have." They're the foundation that keeps everything else standing.

8. Scale responsibly.

When markets are strong, companies often lose their minds.

They overhire, overspend, and overpromise. Leadership convinces itself that the growth will continue forever. When the market eventually slows—as it always does—panic follows.

Suddenly layoffs begin, workloads explode, and the employees who remain are expected to carry twice the responsibility.

That isn't strategy.

That's emotional spending with a business card.

Growth requires discipline. Expansion without foresight is just arrogance with a timeline.

9. Lead with integrity.

Integrity doesn't mean leaders never make mistakes.

It means they own the mistakes when they happen.

Strong leaders admit when something went wrong. They take responsibility for decisions, fix problems openly, and apply the same rules to themselves that they expect everyone else to follow.

Employees don't expect perfection.

They expect honesty.

10. Stop using pizza as strategy.

If morale is low, the solution is not a pizza party.

If people are underpaid, the answer isn't branded swag or another motivational speech about teamwork. If burnout is spreading across teams, no amount of free snacks will fix the systems causing it.

Culture isn't built through perks.

It's built through credibility.

Executives cannot claim to value people while:

• burying them under impossible workloads,
• protecting bullies because they generate revenue,
• or pretending HR can solve problems leadership refuses to address.

Respect. Fairness. Accountability. Integrity.

Those aren't revolutionary ideas. They're basic leadership responsibilities.

Employees don't quit because they hate work. They quit because they're tired of being treated like disposable parts in someone else's bonus plan.

Fix that, and you won't need gimmicks to keep people around.

They'll stay because they actually want to.

Because the best companies don't scare people into loyalty.

They earn it.

Fix leadership, and culture fixes itself.

Ignore leadership, and no amount of slogans, swag, or strategy decks will save you.

That's the difference between companies people tolerate and companies people believe in.

Chapter 21: Conclusion – From Chaos to Workplace

Let's be honest.

Dysfunction is not destiny. Chaos is not culture. Toxicity is not "just how business works."

Companies choose dysfunction every single day. They choose it when they protect bad managers, excuse bullies, reward burnout, and call manipulation "culture."

And the damage isn't abstract.

It's the employee sitting in their car before work trying to summon the energy to walk inside.

It's the quiet ones who used to care but finally gave up. It's the talent that walks out the door because no one listened.

This isn't about spreadsheets or slogans.

It's about people.

Real people. People with mortgages, families, ambitions, and dignity. People who want to contribute something meaningful without feeling crushed by the systems around them.

Work doesn't need to feel like war to have value.

The battlefield mentality has to go. It's time to build something human.

I've lived through the chaos. I've watched good people get ground down by bad leadership. I've seen what happens when companies trade integrity for convenience and how quickly the soul of a workplace disappears when respect is gone.

But I've also seen the other side.

I've seen leaders tell the truth even when it hurt.
I've seen accountability applied equally instead of selectively.
I've seen workplaces where people felt safe to speak, grow, fail, and succeed together.

Those workplaces weren't flashy. They didn't need beanbags or buzzwords. They had something far more powerful.

Trust.

And that's what this entire book comes down to.

Employees don't quit because they hate work.
They quit because they hate dysfunction.

They don't burn out because they're weak.
They burn out because they've spent too long carrying broken systems.

Leaders, stop blaming the market. Stop blaming "this generation." Stop blaming anyone except the person in the mirror.

Dysfunction doesn't happen to a company.

It's cultivated, tolerated, and ignored by the people in leadership roles.

And fixing it doesn't require another motivational campaign, a culture rebrand, or a new set of buzzwords.

It requires courage.

The courage to admit where leadership has failed. The courage to have uncomfortable conversations. The courage to choose ethics over ego.

Because culture isn't broken. Leadership is.

Fix that, and everything else starts to fall into place.

Work can be better. People can thrive again. Leaders can rebuild trust one honest decision at a time.

That's how you move from chaos to workplace. From surviving to leading. From dysfunction to direction.

And maybe—just maybe—that's how we make work worth showing up for again.

And if that sounds idealistic, good.

Every meaningful change begins with someone brave enough to sound unrealistic.

Epilogue: A Personal Note

I've spent a lot of pages calling out dysfunction, broken systems, and the kind of leadership that leaves good people burned out and disillusioned. And yes, there's a lot that needs fixing.

But I don't want to end this book on frustration. I want to end it on possibility.

Because for all the chaos I've seen, I've also seen what happens when leadership gets it right.

True leadership isn't loud. It doesn't demand attention. It doesn't hide behind buzzwords or titles. It's steady, fair, and human. It makes people feel safe to show up as themselves.

And when you've seen that kind of leadership — even once — it changes you. It reminds you that work doesn't have to hurt. That respect isn't rare. That culture isn't a branding campaign; it's the byproduct of how people treat each other when no one's watching.

I've learned that integrity at work isn't a corporate virtue. It's a personal choice repeated until it becomes contagious.

I've worked alongside people who carried impossible loads with grace and humor. People who cracked jokes in the middle of chaos just to keep each other sane. People who refused to let bad leadership define their worth. They're the reason I stayed as long as I did, and they're the reason I wrote this book.

For every employee who's ever sat in their car before work trying to summon the courage to walk inside; you're not alone. For every person who's been gaslit, overlooked, or silenced; your voice still matters.

For every leader who wants to do better but doesn't know where to start — start here. Start small. Start honest.

Because it only takes one leader choosing integrity over ego to start changing everything. One person willing to tell the truth when it's uncomfortable. One person brave enough to model the kind of accountability they wish they'd had.

I've built my career, and this book, on the belief that leadership isn't about control. It's about courage. The courage to face yourself. The courage to be transparent. The courage to care even when it's inconvenient.

If even one leader reads this and decides to choose that kind of courage, then maybe everything I've lived through, every meeting, every breakdown, every absurd "culture initiative," was worth it.

Because work doesn't have to be soul-crushing. It can be meaningful. It can be healthy. It can even (gasp) be joyful.

But it starts with us. With you. With me. With every person who decides that "how it's always been" isn't good enough anymore.

So if you've ever wondered whether your voice matters, it does. If you've ever doubted whether integrity can survive in corporate life, it can.
And if you've ever felt unseen, unheard, or undervalued; this book is proof that you're not crazy, you're not alone, and you deserve better.

Always. Because the work of change starts wherever you stand and it starts today.

Keep doing your best.

-Katie

If this book resonated with you, helped you see workplace culture a little differently, or simply put words to experiences you've had, I would be incredibly grateful if you left a short review on Amazon.

Reviews help other readers discover books like this and keep conversations about leadership and workplace culture moving forward.

Even a sentence or two makes a difference.

Thank you for taking the time to read this book and for being part of the discussion.

~Katie

Need Help Untangling Your Organization?

If the challenges described in this book feel familiar, you're not alone. Many organizations struggle with leadership breakdowns that quietly shape culture, decision-making, and employee morale.

Through **Ember & Oak Consulting**, I work with leaders and organizations who want to move beyond surface-level culture fixes and address the leadership dynamics that drive real change.

If you're navigating leadership challenges, organizational dysfunction, or cultural repair inside your company, you're welcome to reach out.

Learn more at:
www.katiesimpsonbooks.com

Or contact:
katiesimpsonauthor@gmail.com

Sometimes it only takes one honest conversation to start untangling what feels stuck.